Exploring Science

The Exploring Science series is designed to meet all the Attainment Targets in the National Science Curriculum for levels 3 to 6. The topics in each book are divided into knowledge and understanding sections, followed by exploration. The topics are progressive and should be worked through until the correct level of attainment for the age and ability of the student is reached. Carefully planned Test Yourself questions at the end of each topic ensure that the student has mastered the appropriate level of attainment specified in the Curriculum.

EXPLORING
FORCES AND STRUCTURES

Keith Bardon

Illustrated by Marilyn Clay

Exploring Science

Earth in Space
Electricity
Energy Sources
Forces and Structures
Light
Magnets
Ourselves
Plants
Soil and Rocks
Sound
Uses of Energy
Weather

Cover illustrations:
Left *The forces created at the launch of the space shuttle are enormous.*
Right above *A spider's web is one of nature's greatest feats of engineering. It is able to withstand very strong forces.*
Right below *A diagram to show a bridge, with the forces that act upon it.*

Frontispiece *Tall buildings have to be carefully constructed. They often have a wider base to prevent toppling.*

Editor: Elizabeth Spiers
Designer: Jenny Hughes
Series designer: Ross George

First published in 1991 by
Wayland (Publishers) Ltd
61 Western Road, Hove
East Sussex BN3 1JD, England

British Library Cataloguing in Publication Data
Bardon, Keith
    Forces and Structures.
    1. Forces (Mechanics)
    I. Title. II. Series
    531.113

    ISBN 0·7502-0001-4

Typeset by Direct Image Photosetting Ltd, Hove,
Sussex, England
Printed in Italy by G. Canale & C.S.p.A., Turin
Bound in France by A.G.M.

Contents

What is a force?   6
Forces all around us   8
Making things move   10
Floating and sinking   12
Magnetic forces   14
Electrostatic forces   16
Gravity   18
Balance   20
Friction   22
Resistance   24
Flying high   26
Speeding up and slowing down   28
Materials   30
Measuring force   32
Surface tension   34
Nature the builder   36
Across the gap   38
Making things easy   40
Under pressure   42
Bricks and mortar   44

Glossary   46

Books to read   47

Index   48

WHAT IS A FORCE?

Sir Isaac Newton is famous for his work on forces.

Have you ever felt 'forced' to do something you did not intend or want to do? What about slipping on a frozen puddle and falling over, or having to chase something that has blown away on a windy day? We all experience forces constantly. Often we do not notice they are there, but at other times, such as when two cars collide, they are obvious.

What is a force, and why do forces feature so strongly in our everyday lives? You cannot see forces, but you can observe their effects. The easiest way to think of a force is as a push or pull. Forces start objects moving and keep them going. They slow down moving things or bring them to a stop. They change the direction or speed of movement.

Think about a bicycle travelling over a level surface. To get it started you have to exert a pushing force on the pedals and you have to carry on pushing the pedals to keep it going. To slow the bicycle down or make it stop, you have to pull on the brakes. You can make the bicycle change direction by pushing and pulling the handlebars, and to make it go faster, you have to exert more force on the pedals.

Forces bring about changes of shape and size. A piece of Plasticine can be moulded into a new shape by pushing and pulling it. Old motor cars can be squashed into very small blocks by pushing on them with a strong force, using a machine called a hydraulic ram.

This way of thinking about forces is not new. Some of it dates back to an Ancient Greek called Aristotle, but much of it comes from the work of Sir Isaac Newton, who lived about 300 years ago. You may have heard the story of how he arrived at his ideas about gravity after being hit by an apple falling from a tree. He gave us many more ideas about forces, and his 'Laws of Motion' are still used today when we try to explain how and why things move.

ACTIVITY

YOU NEED

- **writing paper**
- **a pen or pencil**

1 Pick a simple task to do from the list below:
- changing your shoes
- getting something out of a drawer
- putting a record on a record player (or a cassette in a cassette player)

2 Make a guess of how many pushes and pulls will be needed to perform the task.

3 Perform the task. As you do it, make a note every time a force is encountered and say whether it is a push or a pull.

4 Count up the pushes and pulls encountered while performing this simple task.

5 How near was your guess?

Forces can bring about changes in shape. As these children bounce, the material of the 'bouncy castle' is deformed by the pushing force of their weight.

TEST YOURSELF

1. What can forces do?
2. What do you have to do to the pedals to make a bicycle move?
3. Whose 'Laws of Motion' are still used today?

FORCES ALL AROUND US

Different forces produce different effects. They are easy to spot when you know what to look for.

Gravity is the name we give to the force that pulls everything towards the Earth. This force causes a book to fall when it is pushed over the edge of a table, and a ball to roll down a hill. It is also the force that enables us to keep our feet planted firmly on the ground.

When surfaces rub against each other, they create a force called friction. The friction between your shoes and the floor stops you from slipping when you run about, but it also makes the soles and heels of your shoes wear out (see page 22).

When two people play 'tug-of-war' with a rope, they are putting the rope under tension. This is another force. The person causing the most tension will win the game. The opposite force to tension is called compression and to exert this force you have to push rather than pull. If you squash an empty can, you have compressed it.

Magnetic force, as the name suggests, is to do with magnets and the pushes and pulls they can produce. The Earth has lines of magnetic force running around it and we use them when finding direction with a compass (see page 14).

Static electricity causes electrostatic force. Sometimes, when you are taking off a nylon garment, you can feel the tiny hairs on your arms stand up. It is electrostatic force that is making them do this (see page 16).

Forces often go unnoticed because they act against each other. A book resting on a table will stay there without moving for as long as you leave it. We know that gravity is trying to pull the book towards the Earth, so why does it not move? The answer is that the table itself exerts a force. This force acts upwards to balance exactly the weight of the book. In other words, as the book pushes down, the table pushes back and the book stays where it is. Of course, if the book exerts too much force, the table will break!

When coal mines are dug underground, special supports called pit props have to be used. These help to resist the forces that would otherwise cause the tunnels to collapse.

ACTIVITY

1 Warm the Plasticine in your hands so that it is soft. Roll it into three identical balls.

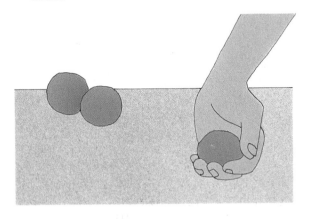

2 Drop one of the balls of Plasticine on to the floor from the height of your knee.

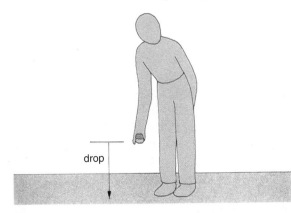

drop

3 Pick up the Plasticine carefully and examine it. What has happened to the Plasticine? What forces have acted on the Plasticine to make this happen?

4 Drop the second ball of Plasticine from the height of your shoulder.

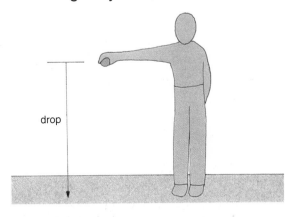

drop

5 Drop the third ball from as high as you can reach.

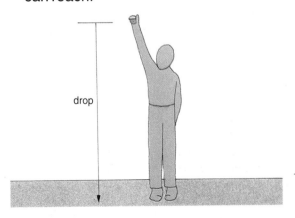

drop

6 Compare all three balls carefully. What do you notice? Why are they different?

TEST YOURSELF

1. What type of force results from surfaces rubbing against each other?
2. What causes electrostatic force?
3. If two equal forces work against each other, what will happen?

MAKING THINGS MOVE

The launch of the space shuttle. A huge pushing force must be created in order that ✓ the spacecraft escapes the Earth's gravitational pull. In space, the engines can be switched off and the craft will carry on moving.

✓ What makes something that is stationary (not moving) start to move? Often, movement is brought about by direct contact. For example, to make a supermarket trolley move, you push it, and to remove a stopper from a bottle, you pull it. In other cases, we use motors or engines to generate the force needed to start something moving. If you were asked, 'What do you think is the most common cause of movement?', what would you say? There is really only one answer: gravity.

If an object has been made to move by a force, what happens when the force stops? The pushing force used to launch a simple paper glider stops immediately the glider is released, but the glider does not stop. It carries on going until air friction (see page 26) and gravity eventually bring it to a standstill.

The question that we started with is a difficult one to think about. This is because on Earth, whenever anything moves, gravity and friction always act upon it. We have to use our imagination and think of a place where these two forces do not exist. Think about a spaceship out in deep space, where there is absolutely nothing: no planets to cause gravity, and no matter to cause friction. Once the spaceship got there, it could switch off its engines and carry on in the same direction at exactly the same speed. This is because there is nothing to slow it down or stop it.

These are the sorts of question that Sir Isaac Newton asked himself. He made his answers into scientific laws that say:

'An object that is stationary will start to move only when forces are applied to it.'

and

'Once an object has been made to move, it will carry on at the same speed and in the same direction unless other forces cause it to change speed, stop or alter its direction.'

ACTIVITY

TESTING NEWTON'S LAWS OF MOTION

YOU NEED

- **a toy car**
- **a ramp**
- **elastic bands**

1 Use different methods (pushing, catapulting, rolling down the ramp) to start the toy car moving. Can you say what forces made it move in each case?
2 Repeat each method. This time, describe the forces that make the vehicle slow down or stop.
3 Can you think of a way of making the vehicle change direction?
4 Look at your answers. Do you agree with Sir Isaac Newton?

TEST YOURSELF

1. What is the most common cause of movement?
2. Which two forces always act when objects move on Earth? ✓
3. Why would a spaceship carry on moving in deep space even if its engines had been turned off?

FLOATING AND SINKING

Enormous vessels, such as this cargo ship, can float because of their shape. This ship produces a large displacement of water, so the upthrust is strong enough to keep it afloat.

Have you ever noticed, when you get into the bath, how the water level rises? It happens because some of the water has been displaced (pushed out of the way). This is the key to an understanding of why some things float while others sink.

The link between floating, sinking and displacement is best thought of in terms of pushing forces. If you have ever had to push your way through a crowd, you will have felt similar forces to those acting on a floating block of wood. When the wood is placed in water, it pushes aside a certain amount. The water that has been pushed aside pushes back, just like the people in the crowd. The force created by the displaced water pushing back is given a special name: it is called upthrust. This means we have two pushing forces: the weight of the wood

pushing down and the upthrust of the water pushing up. If these two opposite forces are equal, they balance each other out and the wood stays where it is. It floats in the water.

Whenever an object is placed in a liquid (or gas), there is always an upthrust, even if it sinks. If a block of steel the same size as the wood were placed in the water, it would sink. This is because the weight of the piece of steel is too large a force for the upthrust of the water to counterbalance.

Why, then, does a block of steel sink, but a steel ship that may weigh thousands of tonnes float? It is because of the hollow shape of the hull. This shape makes the steel displace far more water than if it had been left in a solid block. If the shape produces a large displacement, the upthrust created will be strong enough to make the ship float.

ACTIVITY

MEASURING THE UPTHRUST

YOU NEED

- **a newtonmeter** (see page 32)
- **a large plastic container**
- **a stone**
- **a block of wood**
- **string**
- **water**

1 Attach string to the stone and the block of wood so that they can be hung from the newtonmeter.

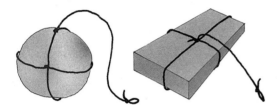

2 Hang the stone from the newtonmeter and weigh it.

3 Leave the stone attached to the newtonmeter and lower it into the container of water until it is completely underwater.

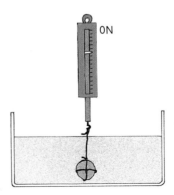

4 Take the reading on the newtonmeter. Can you calculate how much upthrust the water is producing?

5 Hang the block of wood from the newtonmeter and weigh it.

6 Leave the block of wood attached to the newtonmeter and lower it into the container of water. What happens to the reading on the newtonmeter? Can you explain why this has happened?

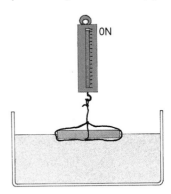

TEST YOURSELF

1. What does the word displaced mean?

2. What is the name of the pushing force that displaced liquids and gases produce?

3. A 5 cm cube of softwood will float in water, but a 5 cm cube of steel will sink. Why is this?

MAGNETIC FORCES

Making use of magnetic force is not a new idea. The ancient Chinese knew about it and used a magnetic rock called lodestone as a simple directional compass. Magnetism is a very difficult force to explain, so it is probably best to accept it for what it is: a mysterious pushing and pulling force that affects some materials and not others.

Iron and steel are by far the most common magnetic materials in use today, but the metals nickel and cobalt are also magnetic. The property of iron and the other magnetic materials to become magnets, or to be attracted to them, is rather special. An ordinary piece of iron is made up of millions of tiny magnets but, because they are all mixed up, they work against each other and so you do not notice that they are there. When the piece of iron is magnetized, all the tiny magnets are turned so they face the same way. Then they work together to create the force called magnetism.

The Earth acts like a huge bar magnet, with north and south poles.

Magnets come in many different shapes: for example, bar, horseshoe, ring and cylindrical. Bar magnets have two very distinct ends: a north pole and a south pole. Two north poles, or two south poles, placed close together will produce a pushing force called repulsion. A north and a south pole placed close together will exert a pulling force called attraction. This rule works every time and you will most often see it written as 'like poles repel and unlike poles attract'.

A small paper clip placed close to a magnet and released will jump the gap between them. This shows that the force of attraction extends out from the magnet. This extending out of the force is called the magnetic field and the stronger the magnet, the larger the field.

The Earth itself acts like a huge bar magnet. It has a magnetic field and north and south poles. It is the Earth's magnetic field that we trace with a directional compass in order to find our way about.

Iron filings are attracted to the pole of a bar magnet.

ACTIVITY

PLOTTING THE MAGNETIC FIELD

YOU NEED

- **a strong bar magnet**
- **a piece of thin card**
- **a plotting compass**
- **a pencil**
- **masking tape**

1 Tape the magnet to the underside of the card.
2 Place the compass on top of the card, near to one of the poles of the magnet.

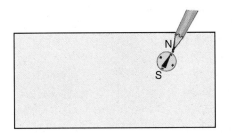

3 Mark the position of the north pole of the compass needle with a pencil dot.

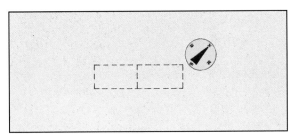

4 Move the compass until the south pole is touching the dot you have just made.

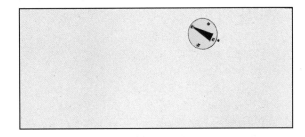

5 Mark the new position of the north pole of the compass needle.
6 Repeat this until you have a line of dots from one end of the magnet to the other. Join up the dots with a smooth curve.

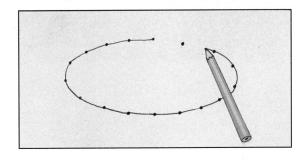

7 What you have traced is one line of force. Other lines can be traced by varying the starting place slightly. Trace enough lines and a picture of the whole of the magnetic field will appear.

TEST YOURSELF

1. Name three metals that have magnetic properties.
2. According to the rules of science, what do like and unlike poles do?
3. What do we call the area of magnetic force that surrounds a magnet?

ELECTROSTATIC FORCES

The strips of plastic attached to this electrostatic generator have picked up static charge from the metal dome. They are all carrying the same type of charge, so they repel each other and the metal dome of the generator.

Electrostatic is a word made from two others. The 'electro' part means something to do with electrical charge and 'static' means standing still. Electrostatic forces are created by electricity that is not moving. This is different from current electricity, which 'flows' through anything that will carry it.

Static electricity is very common. It causes dust to stick to a television screen and lightning flashes during a thunderstorm. It can even make your hair stand on end.

How are electrostatic forces created? Every substance is made from tiny particles called atoms. If you grip a piece of polythene firmly in one hand and quickly pull it through with the other, it will stick to you afterwards. This happens because the rubbing makes some of the atoms of your hand 'jump off' on to the polythene. Your hand and the polythene then have different electrical charges. These attract each other in the same way that unlike poles of a magnet attract. This makes the two substances stick together. The static charge does not last very long, and the two soon become 'unattracted'.

There are many other ways of showing electrostatic attraction. Inflated balloons can be stuck to walls if they are first rubbed vigorously on a woollen sweater. A nylon comb charged by running it through clean, dry hair will pull trickling water towards it.

When two objects carry the same charge, they will repel each other. If two balloons are suspended by thread so that they hang level and are just touching, and are rubbed with a piece of woollen cloth, they will jump apart as the like charges repel each other.

ACTIVITY

YOU NEED

- **a small ball of Plasticine**
- **a long dressmaking pin**
- **a 1 cm square of paper**
- **rods of various materials (e.g. plastics, glass, metals, wood)**
- **pieces of cloth made from various materials (e.g. cotton, wool, nylon)**

1 Flatten one side of the ball of Plasticine so that it cannot roll.
2 Push the pin point first into the Plasticine until it is held firmly.

3 Fold the piece of paper in half and then open it into a V shape.
4 Balance the piece of paper on the head of the pin so that the V points upwards. You have made a simple static charge detector.

5 Rub a plastic rod with the woollen cloth, place it close to the detector and watch what happens. This will occur with any substance that is charged up.

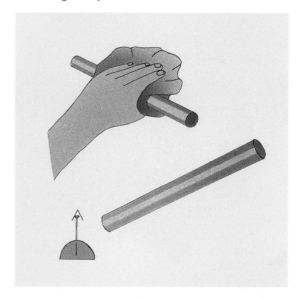

6 Try different combinations of rod and cloth to see which will produce an electrostatic charge.

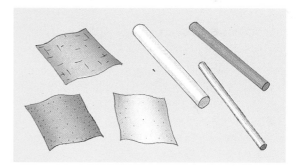

TEST YOURSELF

1. What is the difference between static and current electricity?
2. What is the name of the tiny particles from which all substances are made?
3. What are the two rules of electrostatic charge?

GRAVITY

An astronaut floats around a training capsule, where the effect of gravity has been removed. The astronaut is practising for conditions in space.

Gravity is a force that acts upon us continually throughout our lives, but what is it and where does it come from? If you ask the question 'What is gravity?', the most common answer you will get is 'The pull of the Earth', but this is only part of the story.

In fact, everything that has mass (the amount of substance in an object) exerts a gravitational pulling force. This book is exerting a pull on you and you are exerting a pull on the book. The reason that neither you nor the book move is that the force is very weak. Gravity is about the weakest of all the forces. It is only when an object has a very large mass, like the Earth, that its gravitational pull can be felt.

The Earth's gravitational pull extends out into space, but the further away you get the weaker it becomes, until its effect can no longer be felt. The area over which the gravitational pull can be felt is called the gravitational field, and the pull is always towards the centre of the Earth.

All the large bodies in space, such as planets and stars, have gravitational fields. The larger the body, the stronger the field. Gravity on the Moon is only one-sixth of that on Earth. This is why, when you see a film of astronauts on the Moon, they move so strangely. The Sun's gravity is far greater than ours and this is why we stay in orbit around it. This does not apply only to our solar system: it is gravity that keeps all the suns, planets and moons of the Universe in place.

What happens when there is no gravity? You have probably seen pictures of 'weightless' astronauts floating about inside their spaceship. This is exactly the same effect that someone would experience if he or she went into deep space, far away from any large masses. In this situation, the person would really be weightless, because weight is the force caused by gravity acting on a mass.

ACTIVITY

1 Cut a 50 cm piece of string.
2 Tie the washer to one end of the string.
3 Hold the string up and check that the washer is heavy enough to pull it taut.

If it isn't, add another washer.
4 You have made a simple but very useful device called a plumb line. If it is held up and allowed to hang free, gravity will pull it vertically downwards towards the centre of the Earth.
5 Many things are built or made to be perfectly vertical. Walls, door and window frames and wallpaper are examples. Use your plumb line to find out if the things around you that are supposed to be vertical have been built accurately.

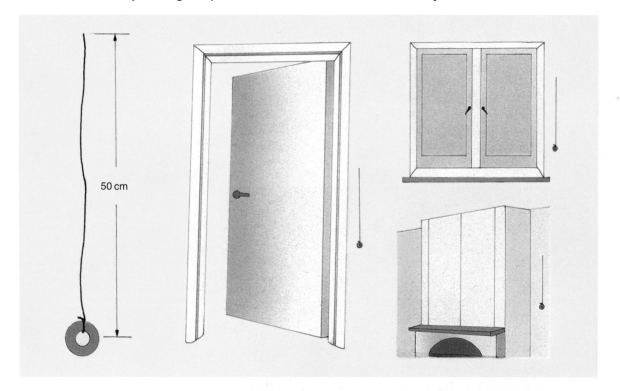

50 cm

TEST YOURSELF

1. If everything that has mass exerts a gravitational pull, why is everything on this planet not stuck together?
2. What is a gravitational field?
3. Why is the Sun's gravity far greater than ours?

BALANCE

Have you ever tried making a see-saw work with someone much bigger sitting on the other end? You probably spent most of the time stuck up in the air! This is because the forces involved are out of balance. Gravity is pulling on the other person with much more force than it is on you, so there is more force at one end of the see-saw than the other. You know by now that if there is a large force working against a small force, the large force always wins.

If you sat on the see-saw with someone of equal weight at the other end, it could be balanced in a horizonta' position. A see-saw is an example of an equal-arm balance. You will probably have seen other examples of equal-arm balances at home or school. You may know them as 'weighing' scales of the type that you put 'weights' on. The forces that make an equal-arm balance move are called turning forces, because they are trying to make the balance turn around its pivot point.

Every object has a point through which its mass seems to be concentrated. This point is called the centre of gravity and it determines the stability of an object. A cereal packet has a high centre of gravity, so you do not have to tip it far before gravity takes hold and pulls it over. A double-decker bus has a low centre of gravity, so it can lean over quite a long way before becoming unstable and falling.

An object's centre of gravity is determined by its shape and where most of the mass is situated. A tall, thin object with most of its mass at the top will be very unstable. An object with a wide base and most of its mass at the base will be very stable. You can test this by trying to balance a drawing pin first on its point and then on its head. Which is the easiest and why?

These children are using turning forces, created by their leg muscles to make the see-saw turn around its pivot (balance) point.

ACTIVITY

1 Fill the drink bottle with water and screw on the lid.

2 Carefully push the head of the nail into the Plasticine, but leave the point sticking out.

3 Insert the two spoons at opposite sides of the ball of Plasticine, so that they look like a penguin's wings when it is walking.

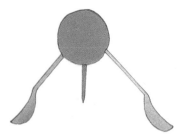

4 Put your model on the bottle top and adjust the spoons until it will balance on the nail point.

5 Once it is balanced properly, push it gently. Watch it rock backwards and forwards without falling off.

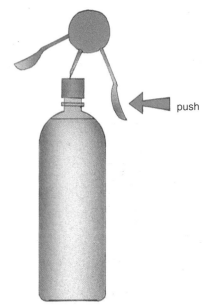

push

TEST YOURSELF

1. Of what sort of balance is a see-saw an example?

2. What is meant by the term 'centre of gravity'?

3. Which is the easiest to overbalance: something with a high centre of gravity or something with a low one?

FRICTION

All surfaces are uneven. Even those that feel smooth to the touch look like bumpy roads or broken glass under a microscope. Because of this, they rub when they move against each other. It is this rubbing that causes friction, and rough surfaces create more friction than smoother ones.

If gravity is the most common cause of movement, then friction must be the force that most often resists movement. It slows down objects that are already moving and eventually brings them to a complete standstill. It also generates heat; test this by rubbing your hands together.

Above *Ice skaters take advantage of the low friction of the surface of the ice.*

Right *Tyres have raised areas of 'tread' to increase the friction between the road and the tyre.*

Moving parts always generate friction. Some machines have so many working parts that they will not work at all unless something is done to reduce the friction. A car engine needs to be constantly lubricated with oil if it is to last a long time and work efficiently. Lubricants like oil, grease and soft wax all work in the same way. They run over the materials and fill in the uneven places, so that the surfaces are much smoother.

Many machines have bearings to help reduce friction. Try pushing a book across a table, then put marbles under it and push it again. This is a demonstration of one of the most common types of bearing: the ball bearing. In machines, metal balls or rollers are used instead of marbles, but the principle is the same.

Although friction is often thought of as being a nuisance, life would be very difficult without it. If there were no friction, how could a moving object be stopped? Brake blocks are made from rubber, so that when a bicycle's brake are pulled the friction produced slows it down quickly. Rubber is also used to make tyres that grip the road, and shoe soles are manufactured from 'rubbery' materials. Surface shape can also be important, which is why tyres have tread patterns moulded into them.

ACTIVITY

SOLES THAT GRIP

1 Make a mark with the pencil, about 30 cm from one end of the ramp.
2 Place one of the shoes on the ramp with its toe touching the mark.

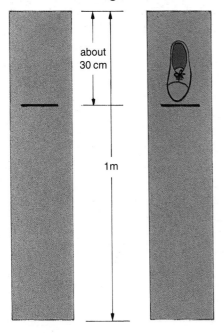

about 30 cm

1 m

3 Raise the ramp at the marked end until the shoe begins to slide down.
4 Hold the ramp in that position and measure how high it had to be raised before the shoe moved. Write it down.

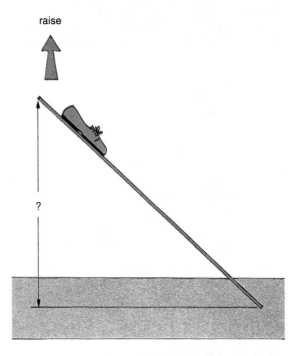

raise

?

5 Do it again with all the shoes in turn.
6 Compare the measurements. Which shoe had the most grip?
7 Compare the different shoes with the measurements they gave. Can you say anything about the soles and the amount of grip they had?

TEST YOURSELF

1. What is the cause of friction?
2. Why is it important to check the oil level in a car engine regularly?
3. When is friction a useful force?

RESISTANCE

Left This hydrofoil cuts down on water resistance by lifting its hull completely out of the water as it travels.

Below This parachutist relies on air resistance to reach the ground safely.

In the previous section, you learnt about the frictional force generated by solids, but liquids and gases also produce a type of friction. Friction in liquids and gases is more often called resistance. We talk about air and water resistance because it describes what they do: they resist movement.

The effects produced by resistance are almost the same as those produced by friction. For example, anything moving very quickly through air gets hot. The Earth is constantly being bombarded from space by meteors, but they do little or no damage because the resistance created as they enter our atmosphere causes them to burn up. The Moon has no atmosphere to protect it, which is why it is covered in craters.

To reduce air resistance (sometimes called 'drag'), aircraft have very smooth shapes, designed to cut through air rather than to push it out of the way. This shaping is called streamlining.

However, cutting through air at high speed is not always desirable. People who jump out of aircraft use parachutes to increase their overall air resistance. Parachutes work on the principle of opposing forces. The two forces – gravity and air resistance – never cancel each other completely. Gravity is always the slight winner, but the parachute creates enough air resistance to ensure a safe rate of descent.

Water resists movement even more than air. This makes designing the shape of a ship's hull a very skilled operation, often involving the use of modern computers. Hydrofoils eliminate as much resistance as possible by raising the hull completely out of the water and skimming across the surface on structures that look and work like water skis.

ACTIVITY

YOU NEED

- **2 m of rain guttering fitted with watertight end stops, one of which has a shallow groove cut in it**
- **nylon fishing line**
- **a stopclock**
- **sticky tape**
- **various boat shapes cut from softwood and fitted with screw-in eyelets**
- **a small hook**
- **a 10 g hanging mass**
- **water**

1 Cut a 220 cm length of fishing line and attach one end of it to the outside of the grooved-end stop with adhesive tape.
2 Attach the hook to the other end of the fishing line.

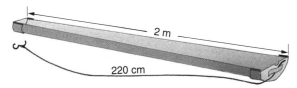

3 Place the guttering on a flat surface at least 1 m from the floor, with the grooved end overhanging slightly. Fill the guttering three-quarters full of water.

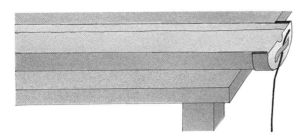

4 Place one of the boat shapes at the ungrooved end and hook the fishing line to it.
5 Make sure that the fishing line is sitting in the groove. Make a loop at the grooved end.
6 Hang the 10 g mass on the loop of fishing line. Set the stopclock and let go. Time how long the boat shape takes to 'sail' down the guttering.

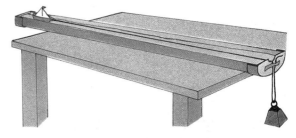

7 Repeat the test using the other boat shapes.
8 Put the boat shapes in order, starting with the one that encounters the least water resistance and ending with the one that encounters the most.

TEST YOURSELF

1. Why are there far more craters on the Moon than we have on Earth?
2. Why are aircraft and boats streamlined?
3. What are the two main forces encountered by parachutists?

FLYING HIGH

Flight has always fascinated humans, but early attempts to fly like a bird were always doomed to failure. If early 'aviators' had thought about the forces involved, they would soon have realised their mistake. Humans are too heavy, the wrong shape and lack the muscle structure to fly like birds. When planning how to build something that will rise into the air and move forwards without falling back to Earth, two pairs of forces have to be taken into consideration.

In order to overcome gravity, an opposite force called 'lift' has to be produced. This is where the shape of the wings becomes very important. If you could take a slice across a wing and look at it, you would see that it has a special shape called an aerofoil. It is curved across its top edge, but the bottom edge is almost flat. As the aeroplane moves forwards, the air flowing over the top surface has further to go than that flowing over the bottom. This difference in air flow produces the lift.

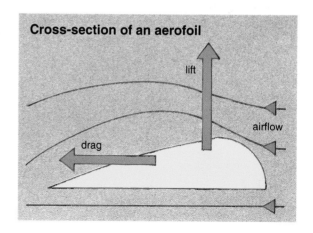

You have already found out that anything that moves through the air experiences a frictional force called 'drag'. An aircraft's streamlined shape helps to reduce the amount of drag, but the engines provide the thrust to move it forwards. You have probably inflated a balloon and then released it to fly around the room. The balloon is powered by the air rushing out, and jet engines of a modern aircraft work on a very similar principle. Fans suck air into the engine and compress (squash) it. This makes the air very hot. When it is sprayed with fuel, the mixture of the two burns fiercely. The burning gases expand and come rushing out of the back of the engine in a powerful jet.

Although air resistance can be a nuisance to forward flight, it is essential to the control of the aircraft. Flaps on the wings (called ailerons) and on the tail (called elevators), along with the rudder, enable the pilot to control the direction and angle of flight. Large flaps on the wings also act as brakes – essential when you remember that a large, modern jet comes in to land at about 400 km per hour.

This fighter plane is streamlined to reduce air resistance.

ACTIVITY

1 Make a simple paper glider by:
   - folding the paper in half
   - folding the corners to the centre at one end
   - folding the edges of the triangles to the centre
   - folding in half again and then bending back the edges to make wings.

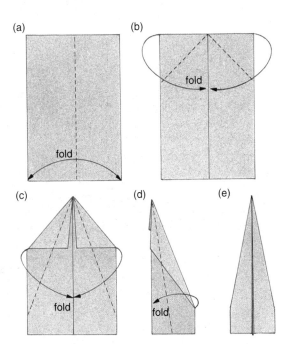

(a)   (b)   (c)   (d)   (e)

fold

2 Test your glider to make sure it flies straight.

3 Make two 1 cm-deep cuts 5 cm apart at the rear of each wing.

4 Fold between the cuts to make flaps.

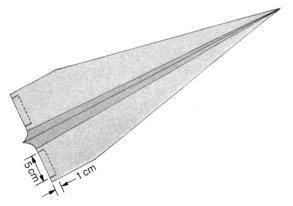

5 cm   1 cm

5 Investigate what happens to the flight of your glider when both flaps are up; both are down; and one is up and one down.

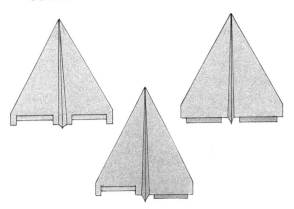

6 Further investigations can be carried out by making gliders with different-sized or different-shaped flaps.

TEST YOURSELF

1. Why is it that a human cannot strap on a pair of wings and fly like a bird?

2. What are the two pairs of forces that most affect flight?

3. How does a jet engine work?

SPEEDING UP AND SLOWING DOWN

Speed, the measure of the distance travelled in a certain time, is something that you cannot help being aware of. Our roads are full of speed-related signs. Those with numbers give the maximum speed allowed, while others warn of hazards that require a speed reduction.

In some sports, speed is extremely important. A motor-racing commentator constantly bombards the audience with statistics: 'That car has a top speed of 320 km per hour', or 'The new lap record is 250 km per hour'. The reason for the different figures is that speed is measured in a number of different ways. The top speed mentioned is the fastest the car can travel, and it probably cannot run at that speed for long. The lap record is an average speed taken over one lap. At some time during the lap, the car will have been travelling faster than 250 km per hour, but at other times (when going round corners, for instance), it will have been travelling slower. A third, less common, measurement is that of constant speed. This is difficult to achieve on modern roads, but it is sometimes possible to bring a car up to a certain speed and maintain it for kilometre after kilometre.

Speed is related to the forces that create or resist a movement. If you have ever ridden a bicycle, you will have noticed that bringing it to a standstill from a high speed needs far more braking force than if you have been travelling slowly.

Another speed-related term is acceleration. This is a measure of how quickly speed is increasing. If a sprinter leaves the blocks and has reached a speed of 10 m per second after 5 seconds, it can be said that the average increase in speed has been 2 m per second for every second that he or she has been running. This is the acceleration.

The Indianapolis 500 is one of the most famous motor races. The cars are specially shaped to reduce air resistance, which is often referred to as 'drag'. These cars are able to reach enormous speeds.

ACTIVITY

1 Set the ramp on the floor at an angle of 25° to 30°.
2 Place the toy truck at the top of the ramp and release it.

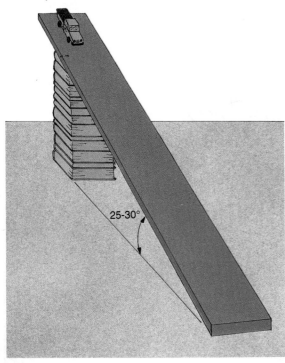

3 Measure the distance the truck travelled after it left the ramp.

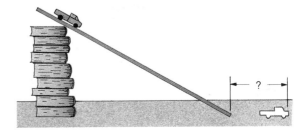

4 Place the 250 g mass in the truck.
5 Predict whether the truck will go further now it is loaded, or not as far.
6 Repeat steps 2 and 3.

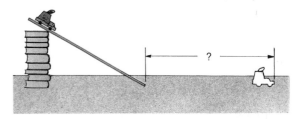

7 Was your prediction correct?
8 Repeat the test with the truck loaded with 500 g, then 1 kg.
9 Look at your results and predict how far you think the truck would go if it was loaded with 750 g.
10 Load the truck with 750 g and test your prediction.
11 From your results, which generates more force: a family car travelling at 50 km per hour, or a heavy goods vehicle travelling at the same speed?

TEST YOURSELF

1. What is speed?
2. What is the difference between maximum speed and average speed?
3. What is acceleration?

MATERIALS

The idea that all substances are made up of tiny units goes back over 2,000 years, but it was not taken seriously until the early 1800s. At that time, the English scientist John Dalton based his atomic theory on the idea that all atoms of the same substance are exactly the same size and shape. Obviously, something must keep the atoms the same, and again we have to look at forces to provide us with an answer.

An atom is made up of a centre, called the nucleus, and tiny particles that spin around the centre, called electrons. Particles in the nucleus, called protons, have a positive charge and electrons have a negative charge. You found out (see page 16) how objects that have different charges attract each other. This force of attraction, balanced by the force of the electron spinning around, gives the atom its fixed size and shape.

The atoms of different substances use the force of attraction to combine and form new substances called compounds. When a compound forms, one component becomes positively charged and the other becomes negatively charged. Because unlike charges attract each other, the two components bond together to form a new substance. If you look around you, most of the things you can see are compounds. Some of them, such as water and table salt, are very simple compounds. Others, such as sugar and nylon, are far more complicated.

Some substances, such as sugar and salt, have a special property: they form crystals. These form when the atoms that make up the substance all bond together in a set pattern. In the case of salt, for instance, the pattern is always a cube. The crystal structure of some substances makes them very hard and long-lasting, such as diamond.

*Two materials that form crystals – fluorite (**above**) and diamond (**top**).*

Below *A diagram of an atom.*

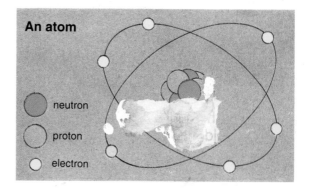

An atom

neutron

proton

electron

ACTIVITY

GROWING CRYSTALS

YOU NEED

- **alum (potassium aluminium sulphate)**
- **a jam jar**
- **warm water**
- **a spoon**
- **a pencil**
- **nylon sewing thread**
- **a piece of fine wire mesh or netting**

1 Half fill one jam jar with warm water.
2 Add small quantities of alum to the water and stir until no more will dissolve.

3 Allow the solution to go cold.
4 Select a small alum crystal and attach it to the pencil with a length of thread.

5 Place the pencil across the top of the jar. Adjust the thread until the crystal is suspended in the middle of the solution.

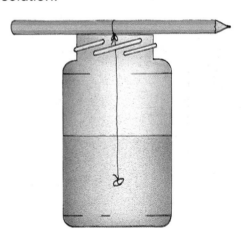

6 Cover the top of the jar with the wire mesh. Put it in a draught-free place that has a steady temperature.

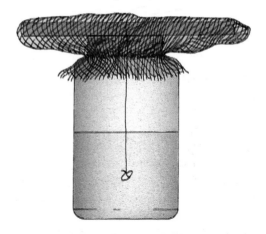

7 As the level of the solution drops, make more and top it up. The longer the crystal is left, the larger it will grow.

TEST YOURSELF

1. .... atom called?
2. .... components of a compound together?
3. Describe how you would grow a crystal.

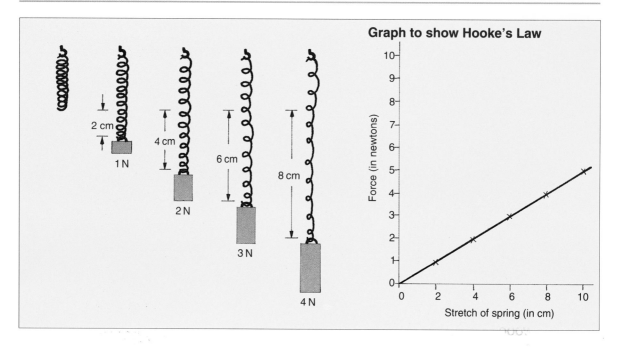

Graph to show Hooke's Law

The name of Sir Isaac Newton was chosen to represent the unit of force we all use. Force is measured in newtons, or N for short.

On Earth, gravity pulls on every 1 kg of mass with a force of almost exactly 10 N. This means that, for example, gravity will exert a force of 10 N on a 1 kg bag of apples, or 600 N on a 60 kg person.

Instruments used to measure force in newtons are called newtonmeters. These are often very simple devices made up of a coiled spring and a scale. A scientist called Robert Hooke discovered that there is a link between the stretch of a spring and the force causing it. If, for instance, a 1 N force causes a spring to stretch 2 cm, then a 2 N force will cause a 4 cm stretch in the same spring. A 3 N force will cause a 6 cm stretch and so on. This rule, which is known as Hooke's Law, will continue to work as long as you do not over-stretch the spring.

The rule also works if you squash the spring instead of stretching it. The common type of bathroom scale has a spring inside that compresses when you stand on it. The heavier a person, the more the spring compresses and the higher the reading. A bathroom scale can be used to measure other forces. Place the scale upright against a wall, lie flat on your back and push as hard as you can on the scale with your feet. The reading you get will be the force you are capable of exerting with your legs. You can also find out if one leg is stronger than the other.

Two terms that people often confuse are weight and mass. It is important to remember that weight is a force related to the pull of gravity. Mass is related to the amount of material from which something is made. When someone says 'I think it is time I went on a diet to lose weight', it really means he or she wants to lose mass. The only way to lose weight is to go to a place where the gravitational pull is not as strong as it is on Earth: a day trip to the Moon, perhaps!

ACTIVITY

YOU NEED

- **a 15 cm coil spring**
- **2 pieces of softwood –**
  40 cm × 10 cm
- **different masses**
- **white correcting fluid**
- **double-sided sticky tape**
- **plain white paper**
- **small nails**
- **a hammer**
- **scissors**

1 Cover one side of one of the pieces of softwood with white paper, using the double-sided sticky tape.
2 Hammer a nail into one end of the piece of wood until it holds firm.
3 Hook one end of the spring over the nail.

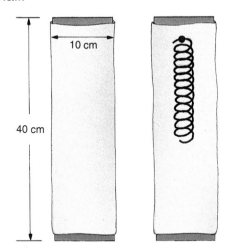

4 Attach the second piece of wood to form a base, so that the spring hangs freely when the apparatus is stood upright.
5 Use the white correcting fluid to make an easily visible mark on the bottom coil of the spring. Make a pencil mark on the paper opposite the white mark and label it 0 N.

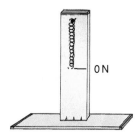

6 Hang a 100 g mass on the spring. Make a pencil mark opposite the white mark and label it 1 N.

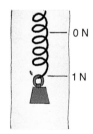

7 Repeat this with 200 g of mass, but this time label it 2 N.
8 Continue increasing the mass 100 g at a time, and labelling appropriately, until the scale has reached 10 N.
9 Now use the forcemeter you have made to find the weight exerted by some of the objects around you.

TEST YOURSELF

1. How much gravitational force does the Earth exert on a 5 kg bag of potatoes?
2. What is weight?
3. What does Hooke's Law tell us about springs?

SURFACE TENSION

Have you noticed that, when a tumbler is filled to the brim, the surface of the liquid is domed (curved) rather than flat? There appears to be a skin across the surface. What you are observing is the effect produced by a force called surface tension.

Surface tension is not a strong force, but it can be important. To some creatures, it is a way of life. Pond skaters are insects that skim across the surface of ponds and slow-moving rivers. Their light bodies and widespread legs prevent them from sinking through the surface tension.

Meniscus

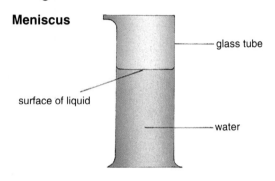

Pond skaters use surface tension to skim across the surface of water.

All the molecules in a liquid attract each other, and it is this attraction at the surface of a liquid that creates surface tension. When molecules of the same type attract each other in this way, they are said to be cohesive.

Molecules of a liquid may also be attracted to the molecules of a different substance. This type of attraction is called adhesion. This is why adhesives are so called; they are substances that attract others with so much force that they are difficult to separate.

Cohesion and adhesion are often in conflict. In most cases, the adhesive forces are the strongest. When you pour water into a measuring cylinder, the level always takes the shape of a curve called the meniscus. This is caused by adhesion between the water and the glass pulling at the edge of the water.

ACTIVITY

A BUBBLE BLOWER

> **YOU NEED**
>
> - **a 15 cm piece of uncovered copper wire**
> - **sewing thread**
> - **washing-up liquid**
> - **100 ml of warm water in a 250 ml beaker**
> - **a sharp pencil**

1 Pour enough washing-up liquid into the water to make a strong solution.
2 Make a 'bubble blower' by bending the copper wire into the shape of a letter P.

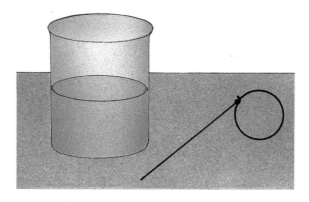

3 Tie a piece of sewing thread loosely across the middle of the bubble blower.

4 Dip the bubble blower into the washing-up liquid solution. Lift it out carefully so that the bubble does not burst.
5 Using the sharp pencil, burst the bubble at one side of the thread. What shape has the thread taken up? What has caused the thread to react in this way?

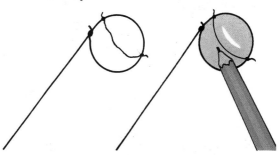

6 Wash the bubble blower and re-position the thread so that it forms a loop.

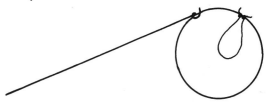

7 Place the bubble blower into the washing-up liquid solution and again lift it out carefully so that the bubble does not burst.
8 Take the sharp pencil and burst the part of the bubble that is inside the loop. What shape has the thread taken up this time?

TEST YOURSELF

1. What causes the effect we call surface tension?
2. What is adhesion?
3. Why is the liquid level in a measuring cylinder always curved, and what special name is given to this curve?

NATURE THE BUILDER

*Spiders' webs (**above left**) and honeycombs (**above**) are two of nature's most extraordinary feats of engineering. They are both able to withstand very strong forces.*

All living things are made from basic building blocks called cells. Very simple living things are made up of just one cell, or several cells of the same type, but most are constructed from many cells of different types. Very complex living structures, such as the human body, are made from millions of cells of many different types, each with a particular job to do.

Have you ever wondered why there are no butterflies the size of eagles, or why spiders do not grow as large as elephants? One important reason is to do with the structure of the skeleton. Butterflies and spiders do not have a skeleton of bone inside their bodies. Instead, they are protected and supported by a hard covering called an exoskeleton. Humans and many other animals have an internal skeleton. This is much stronger, and so can support a much larger animal. Many of the bones of a human skeleton are hollow – partly to reduce weight, but also for strength. Hollow bone is stronger than solid bone.

Trees are among the strongest of nature's structures. Some of them can withstand the weather for hundreds of years. One of the reasons for a tree's strength can be found around each cell. The cells are kept firmly in shape by a cell wall made of a substance called cellulose, as well as by the pressure of the sap inside. As the cells at the centre of the tree get older, they die and form a hard, central column. This then acts as the tree's 'backbone'.

Nature has produced some wonderful engineers. Spiders construct delicate, yet strong, webs across wide gaps, providing the building materials from within their own bodies. Bees build a honeycomb from what seems to be an impossible construction material – wax. A honeycomb is such a successful structure that it is capable of holding 50 times its own weight of honey when complete. These are just two examples of nature's builders. There are many more that construct nests, dens, burrows and traps to very high engineering standards.

ACTIVITY

YOU NEED

- **2 hard-boiled eggs in their shells**
- **a 15 cm square rigid board**
- **a selection of masses**
- **a small triangular file**
- **a small knife**
- **sticky tape**
- **a small spoon**

1 Score around the centre of both eggs using the file.

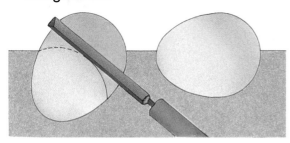

2 Cut the eggs in half, taking care to avoid cracking the shells.
3 Scrape the eggs carefully out of the shells.

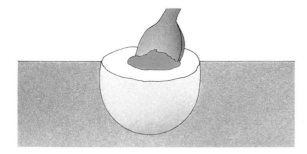

4 Strengthen the cut edges with sticky tape.
5 Place the shells round side up on the table and place the board on them. Estimate what force you think the eggshells will be able to withstand.

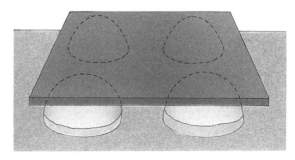

6 Starting with 10 g, place the masses on the board so that the weight pressing on the eggshells gradually increases.

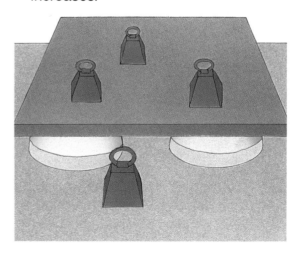

7 How much force did the eggshells withstand before they broke? How accurate was your estimate?

TEST YOURSELF

1. What is the name given to the basic units from which all living things are built?
2. Which type of skeleton does a spider have?
3. From which material is the cell wall of a plant made?

ACROSS THE GAP

Since very early times, humans have used beams to span gaps and to give strength to buildings. These beams were originally very simple, such as fallen trees. Today, beam technology is much more complex.

Many load-carrying beams are not solid, but hollow, shaped like a letter I. This makes them lighter and cheaper, but are they as strong? When a load is applied to a beam it bends, even though this may not always be easy to see. As it bends, the top of the beam is compressed and the bottom is put under tension. However, the middle section is unaffected, so removing it does not reduce the strength of the beam.

The strength of a beam also depends on the material from which it is made. When a concrete beam bends under a load, the lower surface becomes weaker. This is because concrete is not as strong under tension as it is under compression. To compensate for this, the lower surfaces of concrete beams are often reinforced (strengthened) with steel rods, because steel is strong under tension.

Early beam bridges were made from fallen trees or large flat stones. In this type of bridge, the load is taken by the foundations and support pillars. Modern beam bridges are made from box girders or reinforced concrete.

An arch bridge needs strong supports at its ends because this is where most of the force acts. Arch bridges made from stone and brick have to be built over a temporary framework, which limits the length of span that can be constructed. Modern arch bridges are made of steel and have much longer spans.

Cantilevers have beams resting on structures that act like huge shelf brackets. Basically, the forces pushing down on the

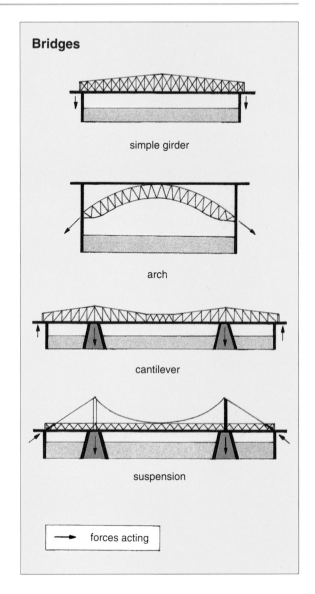

Bridges

simple girder

arch

cantilever

suspension

→ forces acting

central span are balanced by those pushing down on the 'bracket' ends.

Today, large gaps such as river estuaries are spanned by suspension bridges. Here, the roadway is suspended from cables supported by two towers and anchored into the bank at either end. The tension in the cables balances the force produced by the load.

ACTIVITY

1 Place two tables 60 cm apart.
2 Place two of the rulers facing each other across the space between the tables, with a 10 cm gap between them. Place a small mass on the end of each one to hold it in place.
3 Place a third ruler across the gap between the other two. If the bridge is unstable, increase the support masses at either end.
4 Place the toy car in the middle of the bridge. Increase the support masses until the bridge holds.
5 Look carefully at the structure you have made: it is a cantilever bridge. Try to work out how all the forces involved are acting to support the structure.

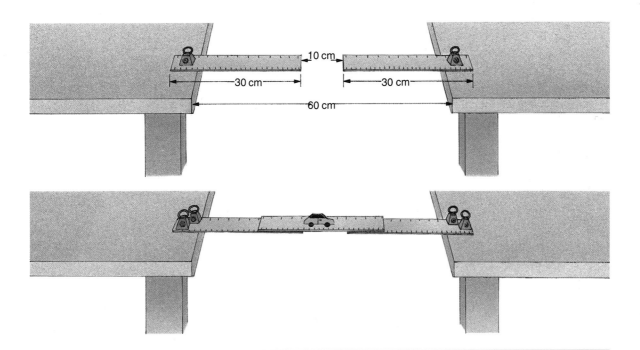

TEST YOURSELF

1. Why is an I-shaped beam as strong as a solid beam of the same material?
2. What is reinforced concrete?
3. Name the four types of bridge construction.

MAKING THINGS EASY

Some machines are very complex, but they do not always have to be. Levers are among the simplest but most reliable and effective of all machines. Spanners, scissors, hammers, wheelbarrows and tweezers are all examples of levers in everyday use.

All levers have the same three features; a place where the load is applied, a place where the effort is applied and a pivot point. The load is whatever needs to be moved by the lever. The effort is the force that is being applied to the lever. The pivot point, or fulcrum, is the point around which the lever turns. The efficiency of the lever depends on the positions of these three features. For example, if you want to remove the lid from a tin of paint, a long screwdriver will do the job far easier than a short one.

There is an old saying that applies to machines as well as to many other things: 'You only get out what you put in'. However, this may not seem to be the case with levers.

If using a lever enables you to get out more force than is put in, something else must be lost. It is important to remember that a lever is a machine and machines do work. The work that the screwdriver was doing did not just involve force, but also the distances moved. At the load end, the force used was large but the distance moved was small, whereas at the effort end, the force used was small but the distance moved was large. The result is that the amount of work done at both ends was exactly the same.

Above *A wheelbarrow is a good example of a lever, as is a pair of scissors (**left**).*

ACTIVITY

1 Place a 1 kg mass at the undrilled end of the rigid strip of wood. The 1 kg mass will be exerting a force of 10 N. This is the load.

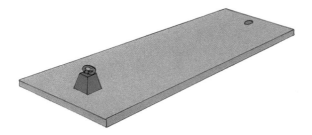

2 Use the triangular piece of wood as a fulcrum by sliding it under the strip as close to the 1 kg mass as it will go.

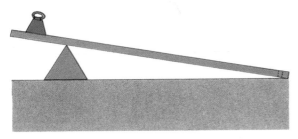

3 Hook the newtonmeter through the hole in the other end of the strip of wood. Pull until the 1 kg mass begins to move. This is the effort.

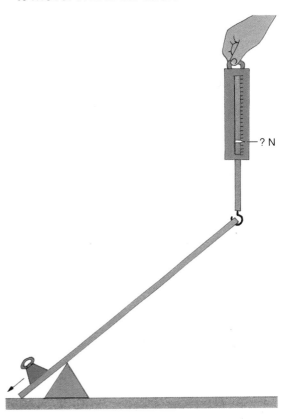

? N

4 How much effort was needed to overcome the load? Did you need to use more or less effort with the lever?

5 Repeat the investigation using different-sized masses as the load. Look at the results carefully. Do you notice anything?

TEST YOURSELF

1. Give three examples of everyday levers.
2. What are the three components of a lever?
3. Explain why, with a lever, 'you only get out what you put in'.

UNDER PRESSURE

Left *Knife blades, used for cutting, are very thin. The force created by the person who is cutting is concentrated over a very small area, so the pressure is very high.*

Below *This boy sucks his drink up the straw by creating pressure with his tongue.*

At the entrance to some buildings, you will find notices asking people not to enter wearing stiletto-heeled shoes. Obviously, the owners fear that this type of heel will damage the floor. To understand why, we have not only to look at the forces that are being exerted, but also the area over which they act. Stiletto heels are very thin, so the total weight of the person is concentrated over a very small area. If the same person was wearing trainers, the force would be spread over a much larger area and therefore less likely to cause damage.

This relationship between a force and its area of action is called pressure. The same force can produce different pressures, as we have seen from the example above.

The amount of pressure is calculated by dividing the force by the area over which it acts. The standard unit of pressure is the pascal (Pa), named after the famous French scientist, Blaise Pascal. To calculate any pressure in pascal units, you divide the force in newtons by the area in square metres.

All substances have weight, so they exert pressure. In liquids, the pressure increases with depth because, as you go deeper, the amount of water pressing down increases.

This is why dam walls are thicker at the bottom than they are at the top.

Pressure is also created by the air that surrounds us. This is called atmospheric pressure and it averages 100,000 Pa at sea level. Variations in atmospheric pressure greatly influence the weather and that is why they are of particular interest to weather forecasters.

ACTIVITY

YOU NEED

- **a bathroom scale**
- **a large piece of cm-squared paper**
- **a pencil**

1 Weigh yourself in newtons
  (1 kg = 10 N).
2 Remove your shoes. Place both feet
  on the squared paper and carefully
  draw round them with a pencil.

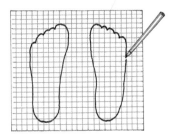

3 Shade in the shape of your feet.

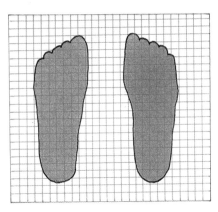

4 Count the squares to find the area
  covered by your feet. Any squares
  that are less than half-shaded should
  be ignored and any that are half or
  over should be counted as whole.

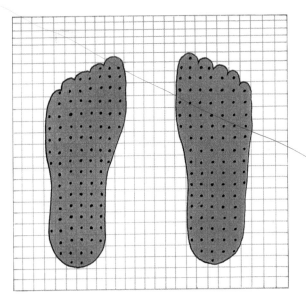

5 You now have the information needed
  to calculate how much pressure your
  body is exerting when you are
  standing upright. The formula to
  use is:

  $$\text{pressure} = \frac{\text{weight in newtons} \times 10{,}000}{\text{area in sq cm}}$$

  (the 10,000 is used to convert sq cm
  into sq m)
6 Can you now work out how much
  pressure you exert on a chair when
  you sit on it?

TEST YOURSELF

1. Why are stiletto heels likely to cause more damage to a floor than flat soles?
2. What is the relationship between force, area and pressure, and what is the
   standard unit of pressure?
3. Why does a dam wall have to be thicker at the bottom than at the top?

BRICKS AND MORTAR

Left *Limestone is quarried so that it can be used to make cement.*

Below *Diagrams to show different types of brick bonding.*

When travelling through the countryside, you may come across a place where a hillside has been cut away to expose white rock. This is a limestone quarry, and the material being removed will be made into that most important of modern building materials: cement.

When cement is mixed with sand and water and left to dry, it undergoes a chemical change. This changes it from a soft powder into a hard, rock-like substance with excellent bonding (sticking) properties. This is the mortar that is used to bind bricks and stones together into strong walls. Small stones added at the mixing stage make concrete. This is even stronger than cement mix. The strength of concrete comes from the crystals that form as the chemical change takes place.

Concrete is used to make a building's foundations, but why does the building need them? If you take a ruler and push one end of it into sand, it goes in quite easily. However, if you try to push it in flat, it is far more difficult because the force created by the ruler is spread over a much greater area (see page 42). Foundations spread the force created by the building and prevent it sinking into the ground.

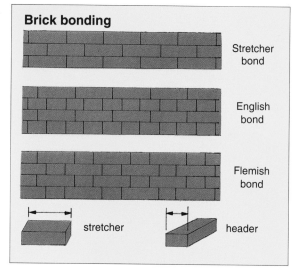

Brick bonding

Stretcher bond

English bond

Flemish bond

stretcher

header

When constructing a wall, a bricklayer will build a layer at a time so that the stones or bricks overlap each other. This is called bonding and prevents vertical lines of weakness occurring in the wall. Bricks are a regular shape and particular patterns of bonding are used for particular situations. The most common is where the bricks are laid with an overlap of exactly half their length. This is called the Stretcher Bond, but others, such as the English and Flemish Bonds, are often used.

ACTIVITY

TESTING CONCRETE BEAMS

YOU NEED

- **cement**
- **sand**
- **fine gravel**
- **water**
- **a mixing board**
- **4 moulds (30 cm × 3 cm × 3 cm)**
- **a safety mat**
- **assorted masses**
- **thick string**
- **an old egg cup**

1 Using the egg cup as a measure, make enough concrete mixture of 1 part cement to 2 parts sand and to 3 parts gravel to overfill a mould.

2 Add water to the concrete mixture, mix thoroughly and pour into the mould.

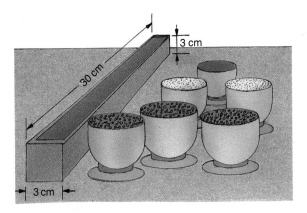

3 Fill the other three moulds in a similar way, but use the following mixtures:
- 1 cement/4 sand/8 gravel
- 1 cement/8 sand/4 gravel
- 3 cement/2 sand/1 gravel

4 Allow the mixtures to set hard and then remove the concrete beams.

5 Place 2 tables parallel to each other, 20 cm apart.

6 Make a strong harness using several loops of thick string. Thread it on to one of the beams.

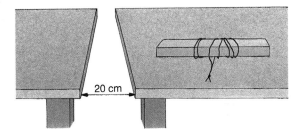

7 Position the beam across the gap and protect the floor with the safety mat.

8 Hang masses from the harness to increase the force exerted on the beam gradually until it breaks.

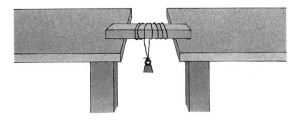

9 Test the other three beams in the same way to find out which concrete mixture produced the strongest beam.

TEST YOURSELF

1. Why is limestone so important to the building industry?
2. What is the difference between mortar and concrete?
3. How does a bricklayer bond a wall?

Glossary

Ailerons Wing flaps that enable a pilot to bank an aircraft in a turn.

Atmosphere The layer of gases that surrounds the Earth. It is held in place by gravity.

Attract To pull together.

Box girder A hollow steel beam with a square or rectangular cross-section.

Braking distance The distance travelled by a vehicle between the application of the brakes and the vehicle stopping.

Cantilever A support structure that is anchored at only one end. A shelf bracket is a simple cantilever.

Cellulose A substance, made by plants, that forms a wall around every plant cell.

Coil spring A piece of spring steel wound into a spiral shape.

Compound A substance made by chemically combining two or more different elements. Water, table salt and rust are examples of compounds.

Compression A pushing force that tries to squash things.

Displacement The amount of liquid or gas pushed out of the way when an object is put into it.

Efficiency A measure of how well something works.

Element A substance in which all the atoms are exactly alike: for example, iron, oxygen and carbon.

Elevator A device that enables something to be lifted. On an aircraft, the elevators are flaps on the tail that the pilot can use to make it climb or descend.

Exoskeleton A skeleton on the outside of the body. This is not usually made of bone, but of a thin, shell-like material. The outside of a beetle is an example.

Hull The body of a ship or boat.

Hydraulic mechanism A device that is operated by liquids.

Inflate To fill with gas (usually air).

Law of Gravity This was first realized by Sir Isaac Newton. Very simply, it states that all bodies (objects) with mass attract each other.

Lodestone A magnetic rock with a high iron content.

Lubricant A substance that reduces the friction between moving parts.

Mass The amount of material that makes up a body, object or substance.

Matter The materials that make up all known substances. These include air, water, living materials, dead materials, stone, metals, glass and plastics.

Meteor A piece of rock that travels through space until it falls within the gravitational field of a star or planet.

Molecule The smallest part of a substance that can exist on its own. All substances, living and non-living, are made up of molecules.

Newtonmeter A device for measuring force in units called newtons.

Orbit The curved path followed by one object in space (e.g. a planet or satellite) around another, larger object.

Particle A very small piece of a substance.

Pivot A turning point.

Principle The idea that explains how something works or why it happens.

Repel To push away.

Sap The liquid part of a plant.

Solution A solid or gas dissolved in a liquid.

Stability The ability to stay in one place and not fall over.

Statistic A fact or measurement given as a number or set of figures.

Stiletto Long and thin; often used to describe the high heel fitted to ladies' fashion shoes.

Suspended Hanging.

Tension A pulling force that tries to stretch things out.

Unit A quantity used for the purpose of measurement. For example, one of the units of mass is the kilogram.
Upthrust The pushing force produced by a liquid or gas when an object is put into it. This force enables some things to float in water.
Vertical Standing upright.

Books to read

Exploring Electricity Ed Catherall (Wayland, 1989)
Exploring Machines Mark Lambert and Alistair Hamilton-MacLaren (Wayland, 1991)
Exploring Magnets Ed Catherall (Wayland, 1989)
Exploring Structures Malcolm Dixon (Wayland, 1990)

Exploring Uses of Energy Ed Catherall (Wayland, 1990)
Mechanics John Freeman and Martin Hollins (Macdonald, 1983)
The Universal Forces Peter Lafferty (Wayland, 1990)
Using Materials Eric Laithwaite (Franklin Watts, 1987)

Picture Acknowledgements

The authors and publishers would like to thank the following for allowing the illustrations to be reproduced in this book: Eye Ubiquitous 20 (above), 40 (below); Geoscience Features 44; Oxford Scientific Films 34; Topham 40 (above); Wayland Picture Library 6; Tim Woodcock 20; ZEFA *cover (both), frontispiece,* 8, 10, 12, 14, 16, 22, 24, 26, 28, 30, 36, 42. All artwork is by Marilyn Clay.

Index

Acceleration 28, 29
Adhesion 34, 35
Aerofoil 26
Aircraft 24, 26
Aristotle 6
Atmospheric pressure 42
Atomic theory 30
Atoms 16, 30, 31
Attraction 14, 16, 30

Balance 8, 12, 20, 21
Ball bearings 22
Beams 38, 45
Bicycle 6, 22, 28
Bonding 44
Brakes 6
Bricks 38, 44
Bridges 38-39

Cantilevers 38
Cells 36
Cement 44, 45
Centre of gravity 20, 21
Cohesion 34
Compass 8, 14, 15
Compounds 30, 31
Compression 8, 38
Concrete 44, 45
Crystals 30, 31, 44

Dalton, John 30
Diamond 30
Displacement 12, 13
Drag 24, 26

Effort 40-41
Electricity 16
Electrons 30
Electrostatic force 8, 9, 16-17
Engines 10
Equal-arm balance 20

Flight 26, 27

Floating 12-13
Foundations 44
Friction 8, 10, 22-23, 24, 26

Gravity 6, 8, 10, 18-19, 20,
    22, 24, 26, 32

Hooke, Robert 32
Hooke's Law 32, 33
Hydraulic ram 6
Hydrofoils 24

Jet engines 26, 27

Laws of Motion 6, 7, 10, 11
Levers 40-41
'Lift' 26
Limestone 25, 44
Load 38, 40-41
Lodestone 14
Lubrication 22

Machines 22, 40
Magnetism 8, 14-15
Mass 20, 32
Matter 10
Meniscus 34
Molecules 34
Mortar 44, 45
Motors 10

Newton, Sir Isaac 6, 10, 11,
    32
Newtonmeter 13, 32, 33, 41
Nucleus 30

Parachutes 24, 25
Pascal, Blaise 42
Pivot point 20, 40
Poles (of magnets) 14, 15, 16
Pressure 42, 43
Protons 30

Reinforced concrete 38, 39
Repulsion 14, 16
Resistance 24-25

Scales 32, 43
Sinking 12-13
Skeleton 36, 37
Speed 6, 10, 28-29
Stability 20
Static electricity 8, 16, 17
Streamlining 24, 25
Strength 36, 38
Surface tension 34-35

Tension 6, 38
Tread 22
Turning forces 20

Upthrust 12, 13

Weight 20, 32, 33, 36, 37, 42